Free Press
and
CENSORSHIP

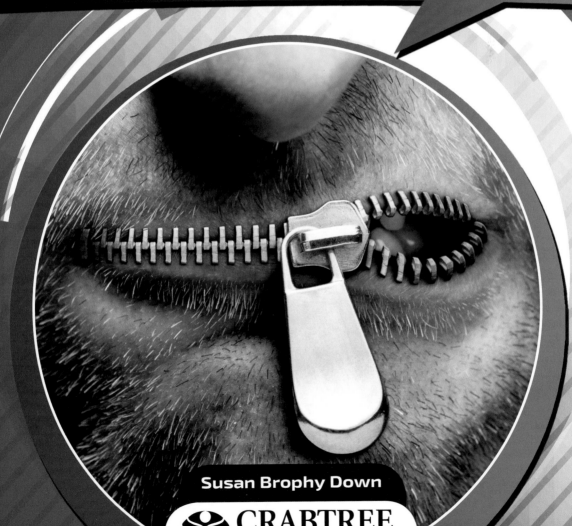

Susan Brophy Down

CRABTREE
PUBLISHING COMPANY
WWW.CRABTREEBOOKS.COM

Why Does MEDIA LITERACY MATTER?

Author: Susan Brophy Down
Editors: Ellen Rodger and Janine Deschenes
Proofreader: Roseann Biederman
Design, photo research, and prepress: Katherine Berti
Cover design: Ken Wright
Print coordinator: Katherine Berti
Photo credits: Alamy: The Advertising Archives: p. 11 (top); Zuma Press, Inc.: p. 23; FEMA: Steve Zumwalt: p. 21 (bottom); iStockphoto: EricVega: p. 31 (website); magnez2: p. 22 (bottom right); Shutterstock: 360b: p. 28 (top right); Alexandros Michailidis: p. 25 (center); Andrey Solovev: p. 29 (inset top left); Anthony Correia: p. 30 (top left); Anton_Ivanov: p. 5 (books); Anubhab Roy: p. 20 (bottom); arindambanerjee: p. 24; bakdc: p. 12; Casimiro PT: p. 28 (bottom right); Chad Zuber: p. 42 (center); Chonlachai: p. 5 (cell phone), 29 (inset top right); chrisdorney: p. 13 (center), 31 (Disney), 33 (top right); Cineberg: p. 11 (computer); CRM: p. 42 (bottom); dennizn: p. 11 (computer monitor); Dutourdumonde Photography: p. 35; Eugenio Marongiu: p. 9; Everett Historical: p. 11 (bottom right); Faizal Ramli: p. 29 (green logo inset); Farid Suhaimi: p. 16; fyv6561: p. 33 (logos center left); Guillaume Destombes: p. 6 (center); Gustavo Fadel: p. 33 (bottom right); Hadrian: p. 14 (bottom right), 30 (bottom right); Joseph Sohm: p. 14 (left); Joshua Rainey Photography: p. 31 (Comcast logo); Kathy Hutchins: p. 40 (right); KMH Photovideo: p. 27; Kobby Dagan: p. 14 (top right); Leonard Zhukovsky: p. 31 (Fox logo); Lester Balajadia: p. 28 (bottom left); Lorna Roberts: p. 19 (top); Lutsenko_Oleksandr: p. 28 (center left); Mario Savoia: p. 29 (newspapers); Michael Candelori: p. 36; NiP photography: p. 6 (bottom); oland: p. 29 (orange logo inset); Pakorn Jarujittipun: p. 25 (bottom); Pe3k: p. 40 (left); reddees: p. 33 (bottom left); Richard Frazier: p. 43 (center); rvlsoft: p. 31 (logos); Sean Pavone: p. 22 (center left); tanuha2001: p. 5 (logos); Thinglass: p. 6 (center top); ThomasDeco: p. 30 (bottom right inset); Thomas Trompeter: p. 31 (bottom); V J Matthew: p. 5 (center); Vlad G: p. 25 (top); Wikimedia Commons: Geo Swan: p. 39 (center left); Goemon: p. 19 (bottom); Kristian Bjornard: p. 5 (printing press); Llecco: p. 38 (right); Piotrus—Gazette De Leyde: p. 10 (bottom); The Central Intelligence Agency: p. 38 (left); The National Archives (United Kingdom): p. 39 (bottom center); U.S. National Archives and Records Administration: p. 22 (center right), 39 (center); University library of Heidelberg, Germany: p. 10 (top); US Army photo A 37180C Bkwillwm: p. 39 (top); Work Projects Administration Poster Collection (Library of Congress): p. 39 (bottom left); www.smu.edu: p. 5 (Gutenberg bible); www.buzzfeed.com: Screen Shot 2018-03-26 at 1.54.25 p.m.: p. 34 (top inset); www.nationalenquirer.com: Screen Shot 2018-03-23 at 1.37.21 p.m.: p. 17 (bottom left inset); www.people.com: Screen Shot 2018-03-23 at 1.44.12 p.m.: p. 17 (bottom right inset); www.propublica.org: Screen Shot 2018-03-29 at 9.58.11 a.m.: p. 32 (bottom inset); All other images by Shutterstock

Library and Archives Canada Cataloguing in Publication
Down, Susan Brophy, author
    Free press and censorship / Susan Brophy Down.
(Why does media literacy matter?)
Includes bibliographical references and index.
Issued in print and electronic formats.
ISBN 978-0-7787-4543-3 (hardcover).--
ISBN 978-0-7787-4547-1 (softcover).--
ISBN 978-1-4271-2039-7 (HTML)
    1. Freedom of the press--Juvenile literature. 2. Mass media--Censorship--Juvenile literature. 3. Censorship--Juvenile literature.
I. Title.
Z657.D69 2018   j323.44'5   C2017-908098-9
                                                C2017-908099-7

Library of Congress Cataloging-in-Publication Data
Available at the Library of Congress

Crabtree Publishing Company

www.crabtreebooks.com   1-800-387-7650

Printed in the U.S.A./052018/BG20180327

Published in Canada
Crabtree Publishing
616 Welland Ave.
St. Catharines, Ontario
L2M 5V6

Published in the United States
Crabtree Publishing
PMB 59051
350 Fifth Avenue, 59th Floor
New York, New York 10118

Published in the United Kingdom
Crabtree Publishing
Maritime House
Basin Road North, Hove
BN41 1WR

Published in Australia
Crabtree Publishing
3 Charles Street
Coburg North
VIC, 3058

Table of Contents

Free Country and Press

Imagine what your life would be like if you lived in a country without a free press. The government could do what it wanted without anyone stopping it. Television, newspapers, and magazines would only show news approved by those in power. Different viewpoints would not be tolerated, and people and the media who spoke their mind would be punished and sent to jail, or worse.

The world we live in has many countries where there is no free press. In fact, there are more countries that have **restricted** media than those that don't. This is mainly because a free country requires a free press. The two go hand in hand.

In areas of the world where people have the **right** to freely say what they are thinking, the press is usually free, too. In areas of the world where the government is **oppressive** or too controlling, the press won't be free because freedom of expression is limited.

Information Channels Open

In 1439, Johannes Gutenberg made his first printing press in Germany. Before this, very few Europeans could read. Books were rare, and in the hands of **nobles**, or the church. Among the common people, news (and rumors) were passed by **word of mouth**. Official news from a ruler was read aloud in the town square, or announced at church services.

As a result, most people were **ignorant** about the wider world beyond their villages. The printing press allowed many books, and other printed matter to be printed at once. More people had access to books and reading spread. Now fast-forward to the modern world, and you can see a very different situation. Today we sometimes get too much information with everything from electronic blogs and **vlogs** to social media and 24-hour news on TV.

We get information through many media channels. Media is the messenger that helps spread information across town and around the world. The media can include words as well as visual images such as cartoons, photos, and advertising. Here are some of the main channels:

- News media (newspapers, magazines, TV, radio)
- Entertainment media (movies, video, computer games)
- Online (blogs, podcasts, and websites)
- Social media (such as Facebook)
- Publishing (books)

Through different media channels, one person, group, or business can reach many people. The media can do this by printing millions of copies of newspapers or magazines. **Broadcasting** sends information through a radio or television transmission. The Internet is another way to reach people. It allows traditional media another channel to present information. Blogging sites and **social media** platforms such as Facebook, Twitter, and Instagram allow individuals, as well as traditional media organizations, to easily reach an audience. Mass communication is the number of ways that a person (such as a vlogger) or an organization (such as a newspaper) create and communicate messages to audiences. Here are some methods of mass communication and what they produce:

Journalism	News media provides people with local, national, and world news.
Advertising	Commercials, pop-up ads, and flyers convince you to buy a product or service.
Political	Campaigns provide information on a candidate in an election.
Public relations	Campaigns inform or influence public opinion (for example, an anti-bullying campaign).
Online	Tweets, posts, and blogs reach specific audiences of followers and provide news, public information, advertising, or public relations.

What is Media and Information Literacy?

Learning to read is one of the most valuable skills you can have. Like math and writing, it is essential to be successful in the modern world. Basic **literacy** means you can read and understand everything from street signs to books. Because there are so many messages coming at you through the media, people need another set of literacy skills. The United Nations Educational, Scientific and Cultural Organization (UNESCO) calls these skills media and information literacy.

Media literacy means you understand how the media works, you can analyze the content, and you can evaluate the results. You understand how to react and create content of your own. For example, when you see a news story online, you might check to see if it is from a writer you trust. Then you may want to send a comment to the journalist or share the item with friends.

Why Does it Matter?

Having media literacy skills can give you research superpowers to find out about issues that matter to you. By learning these skills, you can think for yourself, and know how to watch out for scams, hoaxes, false advertising, and just plain bad information.

Your new literacy toolbox will also help you participate in your school or community. It will give you the knowledge and skills to understand and be able to use your rights in creative ways to add your voice.

Information literacy is the ability to find information you need, organize it and use it in the right way. For example, if you are researching a school project, you will look at books or websites on your subject, write an original report, and not copy someone else's work.

CHAPTER 1

Freedom of the Press

People come in all colors, sizes, and shapes, but they all have one thing in common: they deserve basic human rights. That means everyone is protected by laws about freedom and security from harm.

Freedom of Speech

Human rights apply to everyone. That's why the **United Nations** passed the Declaration on Human Rights in 1948. Since then, the rules have been translated into 500 languages. Most countries in the world agreed to pass their own laws to protect these rights.

One of the most basic human rights is freedom of speech. This is the right to express ideas without other groups or the government trying to stop them. It is also called freedom of expression because that right covers more than talking. You have a right to share your opinions by wearing a t-shirt, making a video, or creating a poster. Some governments deny that freedom and may **censor,** or delete the information or punish you for speaking out.

United Nations
Universal Declaration of Human Rights
Article 19

Everyone has the right to freedom of opinion and expression; this right includes freedom to hold opinions without interference and to seek, receive and impart information and ideas through any media and regardless of frontiers.

> Our Republic and its press will rise or fall together. An able, disinterested, public-spirited press, with trained intelligence to know the right and courage to do it, can preserve that public virtue without which popular government is a sham and a mockery. A cynical, mercenary, demagogic press will produce in time a people as base as itself. The power to mold the future of the Republic will be in the hands of the journalists of future generations.
>
> Joseph Pulitzer

But you can't always say whatever you want. There are limits on your right to freedom of speech, usually when it is intended to harm others. If your message hurts someone's reputation you could be charged with slander for spoken messages and libel for printed messages. Some countries, such as Canada, have **hate speech** laws that make it a crime to attack groups of people in words or pictures just because of their religion, race, or **gender**. In the United States, free speech is protected by the **First Amendment** of the **Constitution**. Some countries also restrict freedom of speech for other reasons such as **national security**, or keeping the country safe during a war.

The right to free speech is limited by other laws such as:

> Congress shall make no law respecting an establishment of religions, or prohibiting the free exercise thereof; or abridging the freedom of speech, or of the press; or the right of the people peaceably to assemble, and to petition the Government for a redress of grievances.
>
> First Amendment, United States Constitution (Bill of Rights)

Copyright
This law protects the creator of an original work such as a book, song, movie, or painting. You can't copy or use someone else's work without the creator's permission.

Commercial use
If a company makes false claims in advertising, it can be punished. This law protects consumers so they can trust the ads they see.

Rise of Newspapers

The invention of better printing methods opened up an exciting new way for people to get news. Here is how the newspaper evolved:

1600s (17th century)

Less than 200 years after Johannes Gutenberg's invention, there were thousands of presses all over Europe and North America printing one-page **pamphlets** of news. Gradually, they were published regularly as newsletters. The oldest continuously published newspaper in the U.S. is the *Hartford Courant* in Connecticut. Its first issue in 1764 was four pages long. The oldest newspaper in the world that is still published (now online) is in Sweden. It was started in 1645.

The world's first newspaper was published in 1605.

1700s (18th century)

By the end of the century, there were more than 50 newspapers in the city of London alone. This was the era of the **partisan press**, when newspapers promoted their publishers' own political views and made outrageous claims against other political **parties**.

The *Gazette de Leyde (Gazette of Leiden)* was a popular newpaper published in the Netherlands in the late 1700s.

1800s (19ᵗʰ century)

Several inventions had an impact on newspapers. They include the steam-powered printing presses in 1810, the **telegraph** in 1838, and **newsprint** made from wood pulp starting in 1845. A telegraph cable across the Atlantic Ocean in 1866 allowed newspapers in Europe and North America to get news from other countries faster than ever. Before this, news from far away came by mail and could take weeks or even months. Telegraph service allowed **newswires** such as the **Associated Press** to carry news from far away. The steam-powered printing press sped up how fast newspapers could be printed. The invention of wood pulp made for cheap paper. This allowed a popular new form of media to thrive. The **penny press** were cheap newspapers with entertaining and sometimes false stories. Each newspaper sold for one cent. Today, tabloids and gossip magazines have replaced the penny press.

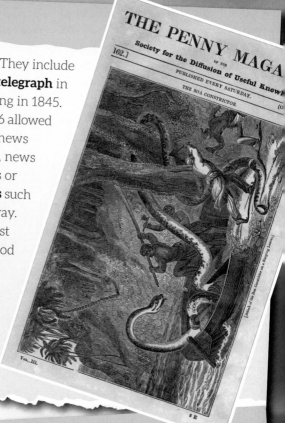

1900s (20ᵗʰ century)

Powerful newspaper chains were created that could influence public opinion. Journalists covered foreign wars. At the end of the century, the Internet became a preferred source for news and entertainment. Newspaper circulation and advertising revenue dropped, forcing many papers to close or cut staff.

Newspaper publisher William Randolph Hearst is shown having dinner with cartoon characters in this 1904 cartoon. It makes fun of his interest in politics.

Rise of the Free Press

The news media has three main functions: it provides a record of the news, it sets the agenda, and it acts as a public representative. In the early days of newspapers, publishers were often arrested after running stories the government did not like. In the U.K. in the early 1700s, newspapers were not allowed to report on political debates in parliament—the part of the government where laws are made. It took a long time for newspapers to be respected. During the American Revolution (1775-83), newspapers helped push the causes for (and against) American independence.

In 1766, Sweden was the first country in the world to pass a law that protected freedom of the press and banned censorship. The country made government documents easy for the people to see, too.

Just a few years later, the media was called the "fourth estate." At the time, countries like France and the U.K. divided society into three estates: the church, the nobles (wealthy landowners), and the commoners. To say they thought of the media as number four shows how important they thought the publishers were. Soon, more countries supported national protections for freedom of the press. Today, the United Nations and others such as the European Union support the free press.

"
Whoever would overthrow the liberty of a nation must begin by subduing the freeness of speech.

Benjamin Franklin, American printer, author, and one of the nation's founding fathers
"

Journalists report on a large demonstration at the U.S. Capitol where speakers are protesting government not acting on gun control.

Newsgathering

Newsgathering is the process of finding, checking, and then distributing the news. Each news **outlet** has a different method. Newspapers decided what was most important, and that went on the front page. In the past, a **reporter** would write a story for a newspaper that was published the next day. Now that newspapers are online, they can be just as quick as broadcasters.

TV and radio news can have live "breaking news" as it happens. All-news **cable TV** has changed the game with a constant flow of news that can be corrected and changed while you watch. You may hear someone on the news make statements in a live interview, but you might not know whether it is true.

Four Arms

Journalists have always been very important storytellers and observers. A journalist today needs more than two arms! They need multimedia skills to tweet the news before the full story is finished, post a video on the scene, and record interviews with people. Then they write and edit. Journalists cooperate even more with the general public on news stories. For example, a driver might send in a photo about a car accident with a comment about the location.

Some parts of journalists' jobs remain the same: they check all the facts and find reliable people to interview who act as **sources** for the story.

Why is it Important to Have a Free Press?

Today, the news media includes other channels besides newspapers, but we still use the word "press" for all of them. That can include online channels such as Yahoo News, and TV and radio broadcasters such as CNN (Cable News Network), ABC (American Broadcasting Corporation), Fox News, or CTV, in Canada.

A free press is independently owned and not influenced or controlled by government. It is a **crucial** part of democracy because it provides news and opinions to the public. In a democratic country, people choose their leaders by voting. But voters can't decide which candidate to choose unless they know something about the people running for election. When voters can't attend events where candidates speak for themselves, they rely on outside sources for information. The media is one outside source. Once the candidates become politicians, we need the free press to keep an eye on them.

DIG DEEP

Should you be allowed to share your opinion on groups you hate? Give reasons why or why not and whether your take on this would be determined by the laws of the country in which you live. If these opinions were printed in a school newspaper or a Facebook post, would that make a difference?

Dangerous Job

Working as a journalist can still be a dangerous job in some countries. So press freedom laws help protect them. Journalists look for and report on news in many other areas such as the justice system (police and courts), schools, and health care. The information they find on our behalf makes us aware of improvements we can make to create a better life for everyone. We, the audience, can take action by protesting, by writing our own opinions for others to read, or by choosing to vote against a politician that was the subject of the news media's scrutiny.

Communication Highlights

1440	Johannes Gutenberg introduces moveable type improvements to printing press
1712–1855	Britain imposes tax on newspapers
1766	Sweden passes world's first law protecting press freedom
1791	United States passes First Amendment to Constitution, protecting freedom of speech and freedom of the press
1838	First telegram sent
1848	Associated Press launched as a cooperative newswire service
1920s & 30s	Radio broadcasting widespread
1950s	Television comes to many homes
1970s	Personal computers, color TV introduced
1976	South African government allows television in the country
1980	First 24-hour news cable TV station, CNN, is launched
1989	World Wide Web is invented by Tim Berners-Lee
1993	First web browser created
1995	Yahoo! created
1998	Google created
2002	Reporters Without Borders starts the World Press Freedom Index
2007	First Apple iPhone introduced

Speakers' Corners

City parks are not only places to go jogging or feed the birds. In the 1860s, people chose Hyde Park in London as a good place to hold protests. Since the groups wanted to be heard, British officials set aside a special area where people could speak on whatever they liked. The only rule was that the speech was lawful.

Speakers are asked to be respectful of others and limit their talks to 10 minutes if there are people waiting. Since then other cities in the U.K. have created Speakers' Corners. The idea has spread to other countries including the U.S. (in Cleveland), Canada, Australia, Italy, and Malaysia.

A man speaks to a gathered crowd at Hyde Park's Speakers' Corner.

DIG DEEP

Can you tell the difference between a fact and an opinion? Knowing the difference can be a valuable media literacy skill. A fact is something that can be proven, such as "the sun is hot" or "JK Rowling wrote the Harry Potter series." An opinion is something you believe, often based on emotion. "That car is ugly." Can you prove it is ugly? Or does ugliness depend on your taste in cars? You can use facts to support your opinion and convince people to agree with you. However, many people form an opinion based on their beliefs without examining all the facts. Some people choose to only look at the facts that fit their belief system. It is harder to change people's minds than you might think!

Is There a Santa Claus?

Life on the Moon! Balloon flies across Atlantic in Three Days! Those were some of the headlines in *The Sun*, a New York City newspaper created in the 1830s that was the first of the penny press. The paper was popular instantly because it was much cheaper than others, so it was affordable for working people. The pages were filled, not with serious political news, but with police stories on crime, local gossip, adventure tales, and completely fictional stories. One of the first editions claimed there was life on the moon. The stories quoted a fictional scientist who said the civilization included animals like unicorns and bison. Another hoax, written by author Edgar Allan Poe, was a story about someone crossing the Atlantic Ocean in a hot-air balloon in three days. Even the opinion pages were fun to read. One article in 1897 was a response to an eight-year-old girl who asked, "Is there a Santa Claus?" The editor wrote that yes, he exists just like love and generosity exist. The editorial is reprinted in many papers today at Christmas.

Tabloid journalism is a style of journalism that focuses on sensational stories. These include crime stories, celebrity gossip, and extreme views on politics or religion. Tabloid refers to the size of the papers.

ASTOUNDING NEWS!

BY EXPRESS VIA NORFOLK:

THE ATLANTIC CROSSED IN THREE DAYS!

SIGNAL TRIUMPH OF MR. MONCK MASON'S FLYING MACHINE!!!

Arrival at Sullivan's Island, near Charlestown, S. C., of Mr. Mason, Mr. Robert Holland, Mr. Henson, Mr. Harrison Ainsworth, and fourothers, in the STEERING BALLOON "VICTORIA," AFTER A PASSAGE OF SEVENTY-FIVE HOURS FROM LAND TO LAND.

FULL PARTICULARS OF THE VOYAGE!!!

CHAPTER 2

Media's Role

People Rule! At least they do in a democracy. One of the earliest democracies was in Athens, Greece. That's where the word comes from. Democracy has its root in two Greek words: demos (the people) and kratia (power or rule).

Finding a Way

Democracy is a system of government that allows the people to decide on how the country (or city or town) should be run. If you lived in a place with a very small population, everyone could make the laws and run the community. That's called direct democracy. In large countries, it is impossible to have every citizen meet every day to make decisions.

In modern democracies, we participate indirectly by electing people to represent us. We do this by voting in elections. People living in a full democracy believe that everyone should have the right to decide how things should be run (well, every citizen of voting age anyway).

The United States Capitol, or Capitol Building, is home to the U.S. Congress. Congress makes laws.

The British royal family today. The Queen is the head of state in the U.K. and Canada. She is not the head of government. That is a position that is elected by the people.

Bike Without Handlebars

A democracy without a free press is like steering a bicycle without handlebars. Neither one could operate properly. In countries ruled by **dictators**, there is no democracy. A free press doesn't exist in dictatorships because dictators don't allow criticsim of the government. Media is censored or completely under state control. Even the average person can't express an opinion or criticize leaders. In those places, it can be dangerous to be a journalist. In democracies, there are laws that protect the media and the right to report on topics in the public interest. If you live in a democracy, you might assume that everyone has these rights. It hasn't always been like that. In history, most areas were ruled by absolute monarchies, which are family groups that hold power. After the old monarch died, the crown was passed to the next in line in the family. That person had the power to make laws and punish those who disagreed with them. People didn't get to choose who would lead them.

This map shows the different forms of government in the world using a color code. It was made according to *The Economist* magazine based in the U.K. Full democracies are dark to medium blue. These are the areas where there is most freedom of the press.

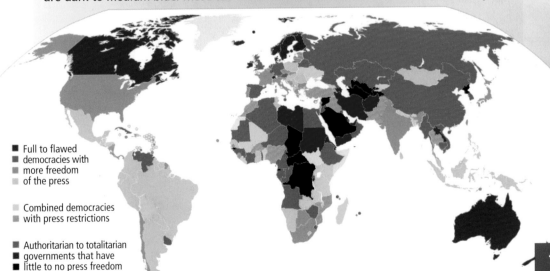

■ Full to flawed
■ democracies with
■ more freedom
■ of the press

■ Combined democracies
■ with press restrictions

■ Authoritarian to totalitarian
■ governments that have
■ little to no press freedom

Road to Democracy

Starting in the 1700s, thinkers and writers called **philosophers** wanted a new kind of government based on **equality** and rights. They were tired of living in places where a king or monarch's rule was law and other people had little or no rights. Later, after several **revolutions** and wars in Europe, some countries got rid of their monarchs. Some were replaced by dictators who were ruthless, and took as much or more power than monarchs. Monarchs in other countries helped reform their governments to allow for elected representatives and stayed on.

There are many types of democracy. The United States and other countries are **constitutional** republics. The president is the **head of state** and the head of government, or highest law maker. Canada and the U.K. are constitutional monarchies. They have a monarch who is the head of the state. But real power to run the countries rests with the elected members of **parliament**. India is the world's largest democracy (by population). After gaining independence from Britain, India held its first election in 1951–2.

> "I disapprove of what you say, but I will defend to the death your right to say it.
>
> S.G. Tallentrye, author
> (*The Friends of Voltaire*)

Thomas Jefferson was an author of the Declaration of Independence. He was also the third president and a promoter of press freedom.

India has a free press, and hundreds of newspapers.

The Will of the People!

All democracies are similar. Even though the majority rules, the rights of the minority are respected. Government has limited power. That means other sectors like the court system can influence laws. When politicians lose an election, they leave peacefully to let the new leader take over. They must respect the voting results because it is the will of the people!

Supreme Court of the United States

Media's Role

The media plays an important role in a democracy in three ways.

1 It informs the public about the news of the day. The events and subjects that media report on can make a difference in our lives. They keep powerful groups accountable by reporting on their activities and asking questions about new laws or higher taxes. They remind the public of promises made during elections.

2 The media creates a public forum: a space where people can share their opinions. That could be on a website, a phone-in radio show, or in the opinion pages of a newspaper.

3 The media tries to cover all parts of our culture by being inclusive. Your local newspaper may take photos at your school fundraiser to show the rest of the community. Media can give a voice to people who aren't always heard. *Chicago Evening Post* humor writer Finley Peter Dunne joked in 1902 that it is media's job to "comfort the afflicted and afflict the comfortable." That means the media should investigate wrongdoing and poverty as well as challenge the rich and powerful.

Media Responsibilities

Because mass communication has so much power to influence public opinion, the media has a duty to be truthful, **impartial**, and protect their sources. If the sources are in danger, they may want to be anonymous (not have their names used in the story). For example, in the Watergate scandal of the early 1970s, writing about a simple burglary led *Washington Post* journalists to uncover evidence of illegal activities and **corruption** in government including the White House and the Federal Bureau of Investigation (FBI). The journalists relied on an FBI employee to tip them off. They never mentioned this person's name in the stories the paper published on the illegal activities. At the time, the White House, under U.S. President Richard Nixon, tried to cover up the activities. Nixon later resigned.

DIG DEEP

Look at the newscast from a TV station (or look at the website). Compare some different cable and network stations. Are the news presenters from different ethnic groups? Are women in those roles? Do the people who announce and report the news look or act like you?

Democracy and Balance

Would you rather eat broccoli or brownies? A healthy democracy is like a healthy diet: you need balance. As a **media consumer**, you may be tempted by **infotainment**, the mix of news and entertainment that many online and broadcast media present. But you should swallow some serious knowledge like world history, geography, and politics as well. The media used to keep hard news such as war and politics separate from soft news such as dog shows or celebrity gossip. These stories used to come at the end of a television news show. They were a kind of wrap-up to the day's events. Today, entertainment stories are mixed with news. News producers, or the people who make news shows, now rely on entertainment to "sell" news stories to consumers. Infotainment also includes talk shows and comedy news shows.

The Daily Show uses satire to comment on news. Satire is humor that ridicules and pokes fun at serious issues so that people see that these issues need to be corrected.

The media should be an **independent** critic that helps inform, and separate fact from fiction. This is especially important at election time. The mass media shouldn't present stories to be popular with one political group or another. Some media are openly biased. This makes one side angry. Many try to be impartial, or fair, in their reporting. But sometimes the most balanced stories make all sides angry.

> 66 So closely intertwined is the concept of press freedom with democracy that a leader must approach any attempt to impose even the most legal limitations on it with great care.
>
> Corazon Aquino,
> President of the Philippines (1986–1992) 99

23

Political Parties

Political parties in a democracy are groups for people who have the same **values** and ideas. The party that doesn't win the election acts as an **opposition** group to keep the party in power in check. That way, the public can hear opinions from both sides. Political parties understand that once they are elected, they are working for all the people. Without a free media, democratic elections are impossible. The media provides voters with information about parties and what they will do if elected. It reports on election wrongdoing. Once a government is elected, the media's role is also to keep it in check.

Interest Groups

Interest groups play a role in informing public opinion and pressuring government to change laws. These groups advocate for issues such as women's rights, peace, and the environment. They will make news by holding demonstrations. They may call on people to commit **civil disobedience** or the active refusal to obey certain laws. They rely on the media to tell the public about these events and the group's goals.

We all have roles to play in a democracy. Citizens vote and stay informed. Groups and political parties offer their opinions, and the media reports on all of it.

Democracies require that citizens get involved not just in voting. Sometimes interest groups can inform the voting public about injustices, or things that need to change. These unarmed citizens are exercising their right to protest in a democracy. The police are there to ensure the protest does not become violent or threaten the peace.

Pushing Environmental Rights

Greenpeace has used the TV media to educate the public and change opinions about environmental issues for almost five decades. In 1971, the environmental group took reporters by boat where the U.S. government was doing underwater **nuclear** tests. Greenpeace knew its non-violent protests would not be heard unless it was able to expose environmental wrongs in the media. In 1975, driving small, inflatable speedboats, they approached a Russian whaling ship off the California coast. They got close enough to film harpooners killing a sperm whale. Then they quickly got the film to the media. Watching the gory, bloody scene on the evening news was enough to make people question why whaling was allowed at all. Greenpeace's then-president called the strategy a "media mind bomb." In 1972, the United Nations had voted to ban **commercial** hunting of whales for 10 years. The Greenpeace campaign was successful at catching the media's attention and getting the message out. The organization now also uses social media such as Facebook, Instagram, Twitter, and YouTube to get its message out.

RESIST
GREENPEACE

People had already discovered that whales were intelligent creatures after large aquariums began capturing and displaying orcas (killer whales) in the 1960s.

GREENPEACE

Check Your Sources

Sometimes people exaggerate or stretch the truth. Misleading information can get circulated over and over on news and social media. It doesn't take long until people believe it. That's why it is one of a journalist's most important jobs to check the truth of every statement in a news story. Journalists do this in a number of ways:

1 They use more than one source for a story.

2 Unless there is some reason to keep their sources anonymous, they say who they are.

3 They contact other experts on the subject, and often more than one. Experts should be people with some experience or accreditation.

4 Journalists should be skeptical. They question things for a living.

5 They are aware of stakeholders, or people who have something to gain by supplying them with information for a story.

Ensuring Accuracy

If you are unable to check whether something you have seen or read is fact or fiction, you can visit a fact-checking site on the Internet. Editors from the *Tampa Bay Times* run PolitiFact.com, a handy fact-checking website. They research comments from political parties and other groups as well as activists and elected officials. Then they rate them on the Truth-O-Meter, and explain why they are true or false. The most obvious lies get a Pants on Fire rating. The *Tampa Bay Times* is a Florida-based newspaper. It is owned by the Poynter Institute, a non-profit school for journalists.

A journalist's job is to give facts to their audience. The audience can then make informed decisions about those facts.

DIG DEEP

The right to protest is a form of freedom of expression that is protected in democracies. What are other forms of freedom of expression? Can you give examples?

Students and Rights Protests

Protesting is one method of exercising your rights. Protestors hope that by calling attention to something, the people in power (government) will listen and change things. Protests are a form of freedom of expression. Student protests have a long history. In March 2018, high school students in the U.S. staged a number of protests asking for stricter gun laws. The protests came after a mass shooting killed 17 at Marjory Stoneman Douglas High School in Parkland, Florida.

Students were a large part of the **Civil Rights** Protests of the 1960s. More than 1,000 young people were jailed in May 1963 during the Children's Crusade in Birmingham, Alabama. This was a non-violent demonstration against **segregation** in that city and throughout the country.

In 1965, the U.S. was at war in Vietnam. Five students in Iowa decided to wear black armbands to school as a protest against the war. School principals heard about the plan and announced that anyone wearing the band would be asked to remove it. If they refused they would be suspended from school.

The students (ranging in age from 8 to 16) went ahead and wore the armbands. The three older students were suspended. Their parents and the Iowa Civil Liberties Union went to court. In 1968, the U.S. Supreme Court ruled that the students were right and they shouldn't have to leave their rights "at the schoolhouse gate." The school board had wanted to avoid any **controversy**. The court said that wasn't a good enough reason to ban the armbands.

Young people participate in a Never Again rally in Florida. This rally and others brought press attention to the issue of gun violence. They also proved you are never too young to exercise your rights.

CHAPTER 3

Understanding "Free Press"

Every day, new dramas unfold around the world. People wake up wanting to know what's new. (That's why they call it news!) They may read about friends and family, and then find out if a favorite sports team won last night. Some people look for news about politicians. Maybe they want to look at a video of a tornado or other disaster.

Public or Private?

Because the news is everywhere, it is easy to forget that someone pays to create it. In some countries, the government funds a public broadcaster. Even though they get money from the government, they don't have to broadcast exactly what the government wants. They are independent and free to criticize politicians. The U.K. and Canada are both democracies and they also have media that is privately owned. The U.S. has public television and radio stations.

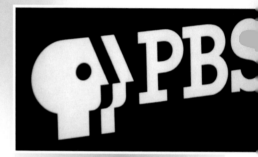

PBS is a membership-funded television station. Its programs, including nightly news, are funded by government, and donations from the public and corporations.

The U.K.'s public broadcaster is the BBC.

NPR is a network of national radio stations in the U.S. It is funded by the public, corporations, government, and others.

In Canada, the CBC is a public broadcaster.

China's Huge Media Empire

With a population of 1.4 billion people, China has become a huge audience for fast-growing Internet companies. Four of the top 10 largest Internet companies in the world are based in China. All earn billions of dollars. Alibaba is a huge **e-commerce** company, much like Amazon. Alibaba owns all or part of many companies that provide online media, sports, TV, and film. It also owns web provider Yahoo! China and the *South China Morning Post*, Hong Kong's most important newspaper. Alibaba-owned UC Browser is used by 65.9 percent of **browser** users in China and 34 percent in India. It is known to leak **data** such as the user's identity and location to **intelligence agencies**. China's tight **censorship** laws forced U.S. companies such as Google to leave. Google is an Internet services company that operates the most visited website in the world. It also owns YouTube. Kicking Google out made room for Chinese **search engine** company Baidu, to grow fast. The world's largest gaming company, Tencent, is Chinese. It was worth $562 billion in 2018. Tencent's social media **app** WeChat has more than 1 billion monthly users. It has been accused of censoring topics in China such as the abuse of human rights.

DIG DEEP

How does democracy make the media more free? Can you give examples of how media in countries that are not democratic is censored? In some democratic countries, the media is owned by just a few companies. Critics say this means that some issues are not reported. Does ownership of media make a difference in how free the media is?

The Super Bowl is the annual National Football League championship game in the U.S. In 2017, more than 110 million people watched the game on television. That's a big audience. As a result, to buy a 30-second ad on the 2017 broadcast cost companies more than $5 million.

Advertising and Media

In most of the world, the news media offers a public service but it is also a business. And your attention is what they are selling! The media try to attract as many viewers or readers as possible. Then they can charge more for advertising depending on the size of the audience. In a print newspaper or magazine, the ads are bright and creative to grab your attention while you read the articles beside them. On TV or online, it might be short commercials that try to sell you everything from toys to toothpaste.

Media personality Bethenny Frankel promotes an air freshener product during the Super Bowl. Companies hope people who see their ads will buy their products.

Some news media online have **paywalls** that block the reader from looking at the content until they pay for it.

The Business of Media

Providing all that news is big business. The mainstream news media (major TV, radio, and print outlets) comes in all sizes, with a mix of information on news, weather, and sports. Your town might have a weekly newspaper that reports on everything that happens locally from high school basketball games to comments from the new mayor. The major media is a generalist rather than a specialist. You can find everything you need to know all in one place, like a department store for information.

Big Changes

The media business has changed dramatically in this century. That's because of new technology, looser regulations, and the growth of big media companies. Search engines such as Google offer new ways to advertise. Rules have eased about how much media one company can own in a city. That means people have fewer viewpoints for their news.

Online ads pop up on websites and social media sites. They are targeted to advertise things the viewer likes.

Newsstands are placed where a lot of people walk by. This boosts the chances that magazines and newspapers will sell. This one is on a university campus.

31

Media Giants

Media companies have swelled from family businesses to huge newspaper chains. Some businesses that started out small and have become major corporations include: the Walt Disney company, 21st Century Fox, and News Corp. Some companies, such as Comcast in the U.S., control your cable connection as well as the content. Sky U.K. is the U.K.'s largest TV company. It includes digital cable and mobile phone services. This media affects what makes news. The news media is often called a watchdog for alerting citizens about wrongdoing and possible corruption. But now there is less barking going on. With only a few owners, not as many voices are heard.

The news media now has more competition from new online companies. This means they have cut their budgets and hire fewer reporters. Many news organizations have closed **foreign bureaus**. That means there is less news about certain parts of the world. There is less time for investigative reporting as well. As a result, new groups, such as ProPublica, are doing some of this work. ProPublica is a nonprofit news source. It has 75 journalists that dig deep and investigate stories that take a lot of time. The stories are made available on ProPublica's website. Other news sources can republish ProPublica's stories if they give **credit** to their source and don't edit them.

News Sources

Knowing where your news comes from is more important than ever. Trusted media brands are good places to start. But where do they get their information? The answer is: **press associations**, government news agencies, tips, and good old-fashioned digging by trained journalists.

Many organizations, including government, issue news releases to the media when they have stories they want made public. In addition, **public relations** companies will try to suggest a story that has news about their client. Sometimes, members of the public bring newsworthy items to the attention of the media. A lot of news comes out of the professional "nose" and contacts that news reporters make. Increasingly, news outlets are mining social media to pick up on trends and stories. That means journalists are reading Twitter and Facebook for story ideas in addition to writing stories to fit social media formats.

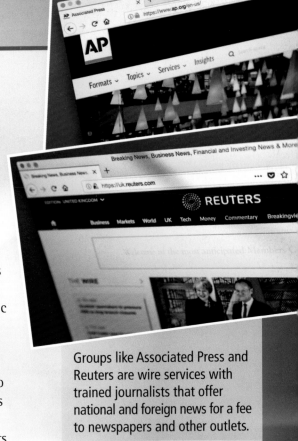

Groups like Associated Press and Reuters are wire services with trained journalists that offer national and foreign news for a fee to newspapers and other outlets.

Hey? Is This an Ad?

You know what isn't really news but looks like news? Sponsored content! This is content written by the news outlet but paid by the advertiser because some companies want their ads to look like real news or feature stories. Maybe you have seen a website link that says "Amazing alien photos!" Or "How to do homework while you sleep!" They know that humans are curious and that lots of people will click to see the answers. Those sites are run by companies such as Taboola and Outbrain.

Watching the Watchdogs

To be truly a free press, the media must be free of **interference**. That doesn't mean there shouldn't be some rules for a free press. Broadcast media has laws and regulations that it follows. In the U.S., the Federal Communications Commission (FCC) sets the rules for TV, radio, satellite, and cable communications. One of its primary goals is to promote competition so that Americans have a wide choice in broadcast media sources. In the U.K., Ofcom (Office of Communications) regulates broadcasters and Internet channels. In Canada, the Canadian Radio and Telecommunications Commission (CRTC) sets rules for broadcasting and telecommunications.

Self Regulation

The newspaper industry has always been self-regulating. But if you see a story about yourself or on a subject that you know is not balanced or is just plain wrong, there are places you can go to complain. Most papers have an ombudsman or public editor who will answer your complaint and make sure there is a correction. Many countries have national or regional press councils that you can contact, such as the Independent Press Standards Organization in the U.K.

Sponsored content may be surrounded by ads from the company paying for the content.

Like print and online media, broadcast media is edited by editors and directors before it is aired on television.

Phone hacking scandal in the U.K.

Competition between news media companies can be a good thing as reporters try to be the first to get a story. But breaking the law by invading people's privacy is not an **ethical** way to do that. The British daily newspaper *News of the World* hired a private investigator to help reporters hack into cell phones owned by the royal family and celebrities. They figured out their passwords and listened to their private messages so they could write stories. At first, the police and politicians said there wasn't a big problem. After another British newspaper, *The Guardian*, kept investigating, *The Guardian* found widespread corruption and proved that hacking was a regular practice. Several people were charged and convicted for the illegal activities. *News of the World's* editor and a phone hacker were sentenced to jail. A government inquiry was held into the scandal. *News of the World* was shut down in 2011 even though it had the highest readership in the U.K. Compensation was paid out to victims of the hackings. Since then, more victims are taking legal action against another newspaper, *The Sun*. That paper is owned by the same company, News Corporation.

| Home | News | Showbiz | Sport | Lifestyle | Video | Fabulous | Print Edition |

SEARCH

NEWS OF THE WORLD
The world's greatest newspaper 1843-2011

THANK YOU & GOODBYE

After 168 years, we finally say a sad but very proud farewell to our 7.5m readers ⬤ See pics & video

Free News Of The World souvenir edition
Own a copy of the paper's very first issue along with a copy of today's final edition

We recorded history and we've made history
From the hot-metal presses to the revolution of the digital age, News of the World has been there

Check out our *Fabulous* site

CHAPTER 4

Censorship and Control

The news media isn't going to win any popularity contests. And that is the point. The news media's goal is to present the public with facts and opinions. Sometimes the powerful words and images can trigger strong reactions from people who don't agree with the facts. Even if the story is balanced, the media often gets blamed.

Censoring the Media

Sometimes governments and others want to take control of media or remove the content. This is censorship, which means not allowing information to be seen. Censorship can be aimed at movies, books, newspapers, and television, among others.

In a country where the government is a dictatorship, leaders use censorship for complete control of the media messages. That way, there is no criticism of themselves. In a democracy, the news media does the important job of informing the public. Laws that protect freedom of speech and expression protect the media as well. Even so, press and media freedom laws are tested constantly. This is especially true when journalists write negative or unpopular news and opinions.

Net neutrality means Internet service providers (the companies that you pay to give you access to the Internet) treat all information on the Internet the same. Net neutrality requires that governments make laws that ensure Internet providers do not block content or websites, or slow them down, to keep the Internet free and open.

Types of Censorship

There are three main types of censorship: direct, indirect, and self-imposed. The direct approach can be violent. In the early days of the media, there were many cases of angry mobs destroying the printing presses of a newspaper that published unpopular opinions.

One of the most famous examples of direct censorship happened in Germany from 1933 to 1945. At that time, the country was a dictatorship. Adolf Hitler and the **Nazi Party** controlled everything. All media was censored including newspapers, films, and music. Books that the Nazis did not like were burned. The Nazi Party set up a Ministry of Public Enlightenment and Propaganda to promote Nazi ideas. All views had to be Nazi views. Members of the media who expressed opposing viewpoints were sent to jail or **executed**. The Nazis were skilled propaganda makers. They gained and kept power by making lies into truth and using media to spread those lies.

In 1837, Illinois publisher Elijah Lovejoy was killed and his printing press thrown in the Mississippi River. Lovejoy wanted slavery to end in the U.S. He published anti-slavery material in his newspaper, the *Alton Observer*.

A Nazi book burning in 1933. Books that had ideas the Nazis did not like were burned in public.

37

State Censorship

Censorship is common in totalitarian states, or countries where the government controls almost all areas of life. The Nazi **regime** was totalitarian. The **Soviet Union** (1922–1991) was a **Communist** totalitarian state that included several countries, or republics. The Soviet government had several agencies that censored different media. The Glavlit for example, censored all print media such as books, magazines, and newspapers. The censorship was so powerful that newspapers were forbidden to print anything that showed the military or the government in a bad light. Books that mentioned food shortages had those lines blacked or cut out. News about western countries such as the U.S. or U.K. could not be flattering. Censors even edited people out of photos, and films and foreign radio stations were **jammed**. People in the Soviet Union were prevented from hearing or seeing things the government didn't approve.

Boris Pasternak had his book, *Dr. Zhivago*, smuggled out of the Soviet Union and published in Italy because it could not be published in the Soviet Union. It won a **Nobel Prize**.

Pravda was the official newspaper of the Communist Party during the Soviet era. It published news approved by the party. Today it is an independent paper.

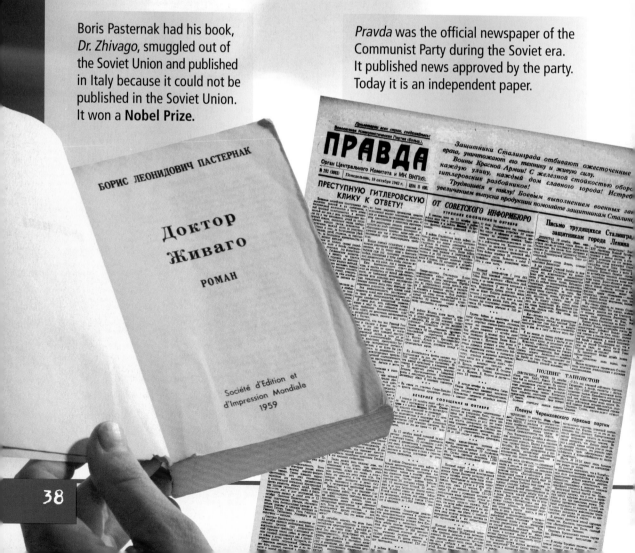

Keeping Silent

Another practice that violates press freedom is called **prior restraint**. This means governments expect to see and approve content before it is published or broadcast. During **World War II**, news was censored by democratic governments in the U.K., Canada, and the U.S. They believed that some media stories would reveal information, including photos and maps, that could help the enemy. The censors didn't allow criticism of military **policies** since it could have hurt public support for the war.

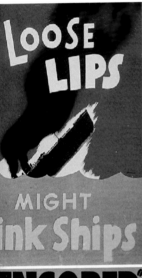

U.S. censors asked media not to report on Japanese balloon bombs floating over the U.S. and Canada in 1944–45 even though they were a safety hazard. Six people died when a balloon blew up in Oregon. The government kept things quiet. It didn't want to cause public panic, and it didn't want the enemy to know whether the strategy worked.

> "
> The first casualty, when war comes, is truth.
>
> Hiram Johnson, Republican senator from California, speaking during World War I
> "

Movie Censorship

In the past, movies had to pass the censor board's rules on morality before they could be seen by the public. For example, in a movie plot if a character committed a crime, he had to be punished. Now instead of being censored, movies have ratings indicating whether they are suitable for children or adults only. Some video games are controversial due to the level of violence. In response to calls for censorship, the industry in North America and Europe created a voluntary rating system, like the film industry, to indicate mature content.

Games and movies are rated appropriate for certain age groups according to their content.

Indirect Censorship

Methods of indirect censorship are not as obvious as wrecking a newspaper office, but can be equally effective. These methods include smearing a journalist's reputation. They also include encouraging people to mistrust the media. Governments can choose to advertise only in media that supports their policies. The U.K. imposed taxes and licenses on newspapers, some going back to the 1800s. They were intended to control smaller, independent publications that held views that **opposed** the government's views.

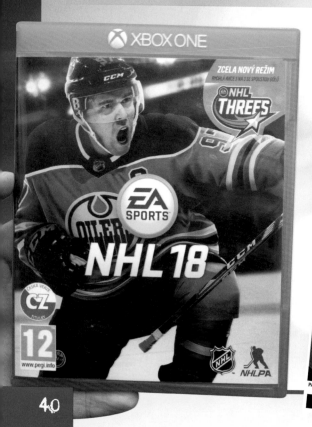

Self Censorship

Self-imposed or voluntary censorship was common during World War II. Some nations, such as the U.S. and Canada, had censorship offices that created guidelines to follow. Sometimes a media company is threatened with a lawsuit for defamation, or harm to a reputation, if they run a negative story. The result is called "libel chill".

The intent is to "chill" the media, or make them afraid of an expensive court case. However, the law in some countries says the media is protected from lawsuits when the story is in the **public interest**. That means the public deserves to know about things like **corruption** and illegal behavior.

SUMMONS

C STOP RRUPTION

DIG DEEP

When do you think it makes sense to censor something in print, film, or online? Consider the following examples: 1) a student being bullied by spreading false statements on social media or 2) a photo of a mother breastfeeding her baby in a magazine or online. What are the issues? Debate both sides of the situation.

Freedom of Speech Limitations

In some countries, free speech has limits. In these countries, a form of speech called hate speech is considered outside the right to freedom of expression. France and Germany have banned any websites that promote Nazism. France even challenged U.S. Internet service provider Yahoo! in court for allowing an auction of Nazi material to be seen by French citizens. Nazism is a very **sensitive** subject in countries that suffered under it. In Germany, it is illegal to produce, distribute, or display symbols of the Nazi era such as **swastikas**. Encouraging people to hate or be violent against an individual or group based on their **ethnicity** or religion is also a crime. In 2018, Germany passed a law that forced social media companies to remove hate speech and **fake news**. The NetzDG law has caused disagreement among Germans. Some people say it prevents people from expressing their views freely. Others say it stops racists from spreading lies and **misinformation** in online news and social media.

> "
> Only a free and unrestrained press can effectively expose deception in government.
>
> U.S. Supreme Court Justice Hugo Black in a decision on publication of the leaked Pentagon Papers.
> "

In the U.S., the First Amendment guarantees free speech, although there are certain limits. The government can't control what you say. But it may be able to curb your speech, depending on how you say it.

Whistleblowers and The Media

When employees discover secrets proving illegal activities, they turn to the media to publicize them. Daniel Ellsberg was a military analyst working on a top-secret report on the **Vietnam War**. He is famous for secretly copying the report known as the Pentagon Papers. He then shared it with *The New York Times* and other papers in 1971. The information showed that the public had not been told the truth about U.S. losses in the war. The government tried to stop the papers from publishing the information. It took the papers to court, but the Supreme Court ruled in favor of the newspapers. They were allowed to publish the information without fear of censorship. More recent whistleblowers include Julian Assange and his group, WikiLeaks. WikiLeaks released more than 250,000 sensitive documents in 2010 to news media in five countries. Edward Snowden was a computer contractor for the U.S. government when he leaked documents to newspapers in the U.K. and U.S. They showed that the U.S. had a huge and secret **surveillance** network to watch people.

WikiLeaks:
GIVING US THE TRUTH WHEN EVERYONE ELSE REFUSES TO.

The Committee to Protect Journalists (cpj.org) creates a list of the countries with the most censorship. They include countries such as North Korea, Iran, Saudi Arabia, and China where journalists are imprisoned and the access to Internet is strictly controlled. Look up the World Press Freedom Index rankings. These are published every year by an international group called Reporters Without Borders (rsf.org). Pick a country that has a low ranking. Who is the leader? What kind of government is it? Why do you think the country has that ranking?

Bibliography

Chapter 1

World Association of Newspapers.
www.wan-ifra.org

Grizzle, A, Wilson. C, ed. *Media and Information Literacy for Teachers*, UNESCO. 2011
https://bit.ly/1UvHZ7K

Citation: Aquino, Corazon. World Press Freedom Day statement May 3, 1998, as quoted by UNESCO
https://bit.ly/2GHOsix

Chapter 2

Tinker V. Des Moines—*Landmark Supreme Court Ruling on Behalf of Student Expression.* American Civil Liberties Union. https://bit.ly/2i6lEnF

Mathiesen, K., *How to Change the World*, The Guardian, June, 2015. https://bit.ly/2J35W7e

Newseum. https://bit.ly/2Gn07OB

Rusbridger, A., *Importance of the Free Press.* The Guardian, Oct. 2011. https://bit.ly/2p7iIcH

Citation: Franklin, Benjamin. New-England Courant, July 9, 1722. https://bit.ly/2JOxzxz

Chapter 3

Business Insider. *30 Biggest Media Companies.* 2016. https://read.bi/1TS72Ae

Columbia Journalism Review, *Who Owns What*, https://bit.ly/2pP3aKQ

Freedom House.
https://bit.ly/2mqxUiA

The Guardian, *Phone hacking.*
https://bit.ly/2pQvSdi

Hughes, T., History's Newsstand Blog.
https://bit.ly/2GBhP5X

Maheshwari, S., *$5 Million for Super Bowl Ad.* New York Times, Jan. 2017. https://nyti.ms/2jIMUIx

Ofcom, U.K. https://bit.ly/2uABIFA

United Nations, Universal Declaration of Human Rights, Article 19, Dec. 1948. https://bit.ly/1O8f0nS

Chapter 4

Beacon for Freedom. https://bit.ly/2pPOVWd

Canadian Journalists for Free Expression.
www.cjfe.org

Committee to Protect Journalists, Most Censored Countries. https://bit.ly/1JqHwxu

Freedom House. https://bit.ly/2mqxUiA

IFEX, International Freedom of Expression Exchange. https://ifex.org

Mikesh, R. *Japanese Balloon Bomb Attacks,* Smithsonian Institution Press. 1973. https://library.uoregon.edu/ec/e-asia/read/balloon.pdf

Reporters without Borders, Index of Press Freedom. https://bit.ly/2GkWZ7p

Spartacus Educational, Elijah Lovejoy.
https://bit.ly/2GWozsL

U.S. Supreme Court (Justice Hugo Black). Decision in case of New York Times Co. v. United States, June 1971. https://bit.ly/2iVWGoz

Learning More

Books

Donovan, Sandy, *Media, From News Coverage to Political Advertising*, Lerner Publishing, 2016.

Paiser, Barb, *Choosing News: What Gets Reported and Why*. Capstone Publishing, 2012.

Websites

The American Press Institute has activities on understanding media.
www.americanpressinstitute.org/wp-content/uploads/2013/10/Introductory-News-Literacy-curriculum.pdf

The International Free Expression Exchange runs an information service on examples of censorship from around the world.
https://ifex.org

The Newseum is a museum located in Washington that offers some thoughtful activities to help people understand the media's handling of current events.
https://newseumed.org/ed-tools/#?

Reporters Without Borders gathers statistics and creates the annual World Press Freedom ratings.
https://rsf.org/en/ranking

PolitiFact is a creative rating of truth or fiction from politicians.
www.politifact.com

Public Broadcasting Services (PBS) has lesson plans on media literacy and documentary films.
PBS show POV
www.pbs.org/pov/behindthelens/lesson-plan-1
PBS Newshour
www.pbs.org/newshour/extra/tag/media-literacy

Glossary

app An application for mobile phones

Associated Press A co-operative news agency owned by a number of newspapers and radio and television stations that agree to contribute and share stories that would be difficult for just one news organization to get on its own

attributed Regarded as belonging or having come from a specific person or thing

broadcasting Something that is transmitted on television or radio

browser Software program that allows the user to find and read encoded documents on the Internet

cable TV Television transmission by means of a cable, as opposed to network TV, which transmits radio waves through the air

censor To suppress information in all forms of media

censorship Not allowing news or information to be released to the general public. Stopping news, images, books, or movies from freely sharing information

civil disobedience The active refusal to obey a law or command that a person thinks is morally wrong

civil liberty Legal rights of the individual

civil rights Full legal, social, and economic equality for minority groups

constitution A document prepared by the government that sets up the ideas that it stands for and how a country will be governed

constitutional Subject to the laws of the constitution

controversy Something that is disputed or the cause of disagreement

corruption Dishonest actions, particularly in business and government

credit Honors given for action

data Facts and information intended to be studied to find something out

dictator A person or leader who rules with absolute control and power

direct democracy A system that allows citizens full participation in decision-making

e-commerce Buying or selling something online or over the Internet

equality Being equal in rank, value, position, or ability

ethnicity An ethnic group, its traits or background that people belong to

executed Killed or murdered, or brought something to an end

fake news A type of journalism or propaganda that deliberately misinforms

First Amendment An amendment, or addition, to the U.S. Constitution that makes up part of the Bill of Rights that all Americans have. It prevents the government from blocking freedom of religion, speech, expression, or assembly

foreign bureaus News organization offices in different countries than the head office of the organization

gender The characteristics society gives to people based on their sex

hate speech Speech that is intended to cause a group of people to attack another based on a number of things including race, ethnicity, religion, gender, or disability

head of state The person who represents the state in a national government

ignorant Lacking in knowledge or unaware

impartial Something that is fair and just and not biased

independent Something not influenced or controlled by the opinions and behavior of others

infotainment Television or radio programs that dramatize facts to make them understandable as entertainment

intelligence agencies Government departments that get information on people, foreign governments, or other armed forces

interest groups A group or community that has a specific interest such as animal rights or children's rights, and tries to influence the government to make laws and policies that benefit these interests

interference Preventing someone from doing something or hearing something

jammed Blocked radio and television signals so that people cannot hear them

literacy Knowledge of a certain subject and the ability to "read" or interpret meaning

media consumer A person who watches, reads, or listens to media

misinformation Giving false or misleading information

Glossary

monarch A ruler such as a king or queen who inherits the position through family ties and is the head of the country

Nazi Party A political party in Germany that came to lead the country (1933–1945). The Nazi Party is known for its racist policies, mass killings, and aggression that led to World War II

newsprint A type of paper made from wood pulp used mostly for newspapers

newswires A service transmitted at first by teletypewriter and now via computer where news stories are shared

Nobel Prize Awards given each year for outstanding achievement in areas of science, literature, and peace

nobles The wealthy class who inherited their positions many centuries ago

nuclear Relating to nuclear weapons or power

opposed Resisting or standing in the way of something

opposition A person or group of people who oppose or protest something

oppressive Overly harsh and controlling

pamphlets Printed information or essays on a topic

parliament The legislative part of government in several countries around the world, including Canada and the U.K.

Partisan press Newspapers that openly support a specific political party and follow the party's agenda

paywalls Part of a website that can only be seen by people who pay to see it

penny press Cheap, mass market newspapers produced in the United States from the 1830s-on

policies Government courses of action

political parties Organized groups of people who have the same aims and world views and seek to influence the way the government works by getting elected to government

press associations Groups for journalists that work on their behalf and help protect the public's right to know

prior restraint A type of censorship that bans certain communication before it happens

public interest The well-being of the general public

regime A government in power

reporter A person who reports news for newspapers, radio, television, or online

restricted Something that is limited, either in scope or size

revolution The overthrow of an existing government and replacement with a new one

right The freedoms or fundamental human rights that belong to everyone but are denied in some countries

search engine A computer program that searches documents on the Internet using specific keywords

segregation The laws and practices that set black people apart from white people in all areas of life including schools and transportation

sensitive Especially affected or pained by something

social media Communication channels such as Facebook, Instagram, and Twitter that are used by large groups of people to share information

Soviet Union A union of 15 different republics in eastern Europe and western Asia that were under Communist rule from 1922–1991

surveillance Keeping watch over someone or something

swastika An ancient symbol of an equal-armed cross that was adopted as a symbol of the Nazi Party in Germany

tabloids Publications that are smaller in size than standard newspaper and often contain more sensationalized stories

telegraph A system for transmitting messages by signal from distant places. Telegraphs were widely used before the telephone was invented

values The things, including behavior and ways of life, a person or a society believes in

Vietnam War A conflct in Vietnam that began in 1954 and ended in 1975 that caused millions of deaths and involved many countries including the United States, Australia, South Vietnam, and North Vietnam

vlogs A video blog with opinions or observations from its creator

whistleblower A person who informs others about an illegal or unethical activity, sometimes at great risk to themselves

word of mouth Information passed from person to person verbally, or through talking

World War II A major war from 1939–1945 between the Allies, including Britain, France and the Axis powers of Germany, Italy, Japan and their allies

Index

About the Author

Susan Brophy Down is a former marketing manager and newspaper writer who has published four other books for youth. Even though she knows how advertising works on the emotions, some commercials can still make her cry.